Fall in love with the Mass...

Fall in love with Jesus! ♡

Sam Freidhoff

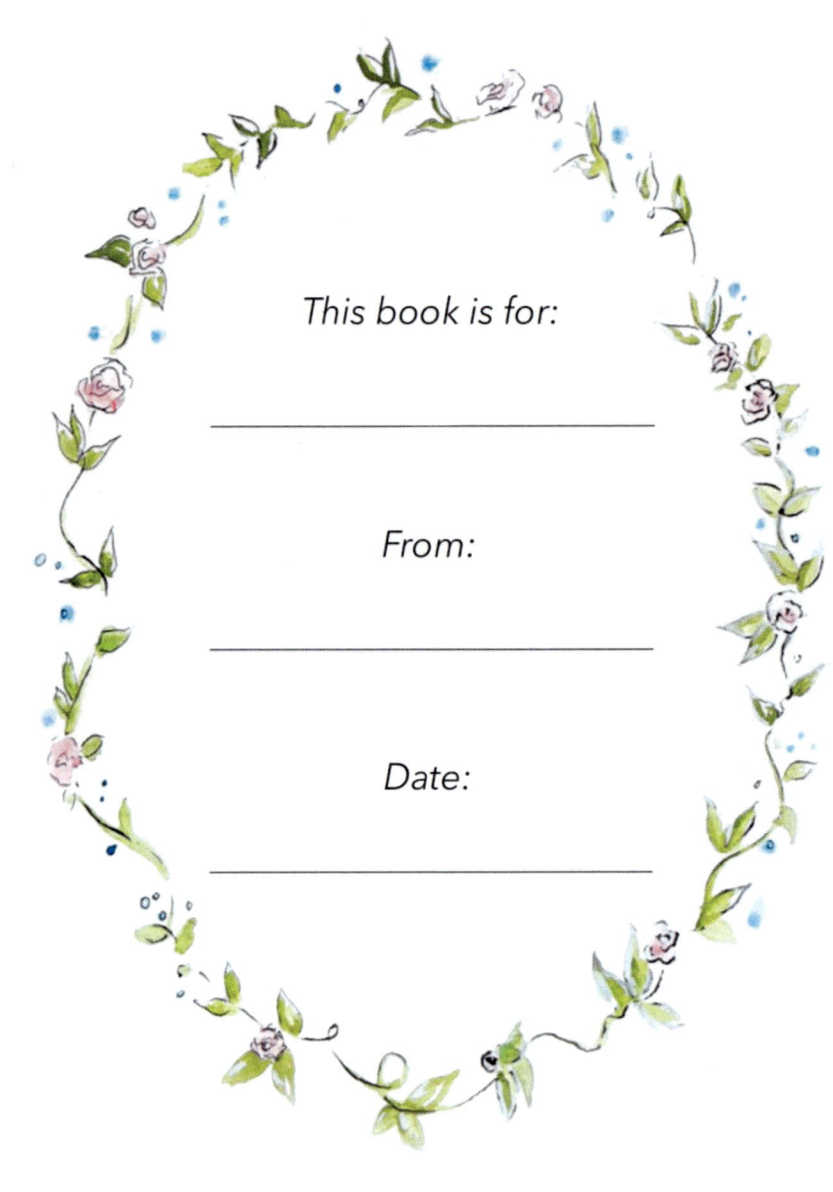

This book is for:

_____

From:

_____

Date:

_____

Discover the Faith Series
Discover the Gestures of the Mass

By **Pam Freidhoff**
Illustrated by **Monica Morel**

Copyright © 2023. All Rights Reserved.

May not be copied or reproduced without written permission from the author and artist.

ACKNOWLEDGMENTS

The author would like to acknowledge all her collaborators:

Deacon Carl Freidhoff,
Carol and Joe Morel,
Alex Daley, Tracy Noll,
Diane Skirpan,
Fr. Sylvan Capitani,
and all who helped in her formation
through the Catechesis of the Good Shepherd.

The artist would like to thank:

S. Jacqueline Gold at *John Paul the Great Catholic University* for
her education and guidance through the illustration process,
and
Dr. David Appleby and all the Tutors and Faculty
at *Thomas Aquinas College* who encouraged her artistic pursuits.

This book is dedicated to you,
God's precious child.

As we enter our Church,
we make the **Sign of the Cross**
calling to mind our Baptism.

We bless ourselves in the name
of the Father,
and the Son,
and the Holy Spirit.
Amen.

Make the **Sign of the Cross**
by using your right hand to touch
your forehead, chest,
left shoulder, and right shoulder.

We **Genuflect** to the tabernacle
where the Eucharist is kept.

This shows Jesus,
King of Kings
and
Lord of Lords,
our profound respect.

Genuflect by bending your right knee and
letting it touch the ground.

The priest adds water
to the wine
in the **Preparation of the Chalice**.

The wine will become Jesus.
The drop of water
represents us.

What happens to the water
when it is added to the wine?
Can they be separated?

The priest prepares for the Eucharist
by cleansing his hands,
and his heart, too.

We silently ask God to purify our hearts
as we ask for forgiveness
from our pew.

Show how the priest does the gesture of
the **Washing of the Hands**.

At the **Epiclesis** the priest extends
his hands above the gifts of
bread and wine.

The power of the Holy Spirit comes down
so they can become
the Sacrament Divine.

Show with your hands
how the priest invokes the Holy Spirit
during the **Epiclesis**.

The priest lifts up
Jesus' Body and Blood
in the **Offering** and will pray.

We are part of this offering
and affirm it
as the "Great Amen" we say.

Show with your hands how the priest
elevates the Body and Blood of Jesus
in the **Offering**.

We receive God's Love
through the Epiclesis
and respond through the Offering,
you recall.

Now is the time for
the **Sign of Peace**
to extend God's peace
and love to all.

Offer the **Sign of Peace**
to your neighbor with the words,
"The peace of the Lord be with you."

The Mass is a marvelous gift
God has given us
from above.

As the Mass comes to an end,
we are sent forth
to spread God's love.

Read Along! Sing Along!

This book includes links to both an audio Read-Along
and a beautiful Sing-Along version –
performed by Diane Skirpan.

**Scan for
Read-Along**

Or visit online at:
https://youtu.be/0zzdwUCdOSw

**Scan for
Sing-Along**

Or visit online at:
https://youtu.be/3YGT8tJQwLc

Made in the USA
Middletown, DE
28 August 2023